THE OFFICIAL
ARSENAL
ANNUAL
2021

Written by Josh James
Designed by Adam Wilsher

A Grange Publication

Manufactured and distributed under licence by Grange Communications Ltd., Edinburgh. Printed in the EU.

Photographs © Arsenal Football Club, PA Images and Shutterstock.

ISBN 978-1-913034-86-3

CONTENTS

Welcome to the Official Arsenal Annual 2021.

What a fantastic end to the season we had in August!

It was the most crazy season any of us have ever known, but for me it will forever live in my memory as the time that I was privileged enough to take up the position of head coach at this famous football club.

It was a huge honour to take charge last December, and to end my first year back here with some silverware for the supporters was an absolute dream for me. It's just a shame that our fantastic fans weren't able to be with us at Wembley on the day, but we know you were right behind us, wherever in the world you watched it. This one is for you.

But I also know that this is just the start. I have had the most incredible reception ever since I came back to the club and I know exactly what the demands of the supporters and everybody at the club are.

I have those same ambitions, and I want us all to be proud of this club, to all be together, and to keep improving all the time to move Arsenal forward.

We have a lot of work to do with that, and the players know what I expect from them. We have certain behaviours and demands that are absolutely non-negotiable. Things that I expect to see from my team whenever they wear our club colours - both in training and in matches.

We have a clear process here, which we all need to trust. If we do, I am confident that we can achieve great things together. That is my mission: to make everybody - players, staff, supporters - believe in where we can go, and then deliver it.

So enjoy the book, thanks for your amazing support, and come on you Gunners!

MIKEL ARTETA

ROLL OF HONOUR

League champions:
1931, 1933, 1934, 1935, 1938, 1948, 1953, 1971, 1989, 1991, 1998, 2002, 2004
FA Cup winners:
1930, 1936, 1950, 1971, 1979, 1993, 1998, 2002, 2003, 2005, 2014, 2015, 2017, 2020
League Cup winners:
1987, 1993
European Fairs Cup winners: 1970
European Cup Winners' Cup winners: 1994
Charity/Community Shield winners: 1930, 1931, 1933, 1934, 1938, 1948, 1953, 1991 (shared), 1998, 1999, 2002, 2004, 2014, 2015, 2017, 2020

SEASON REVIEW

AUGUST

Pierre-Emerick Aubameyang picked up where he left off the previous season, scoring the only goal in our opening weekend win away to Newcastle United. New signings Nicolas Pepe, Dani Ceballos and Gabriel Martinelli were all involved for their Gunners debuts, as we recorded a clean sheet on the road in the Premier League - something we managed only once in the whole of the previous campaign.

New midfielder Ceballos was particularly impressive in our first home game – a 2-1 victory over Burnley – and it was the familiar names of Aubameyang and Alexandre Lacazette on the scoresheet. The month ended with our first defeat of the season though, Lucas Torreira's late strike proving no more than a consolation in a 3-1 reverse at Anfield.

RESULTS

Sun 11 Premier League
Newcastle United (A)
1-0 *Aubameyang*

Sat 17 Premier League
Burnley (H)
2-1 *Lacazette, Aubameyang*

Sat 24 Premier League
Liverpool (A)
1-3 *Torreira*

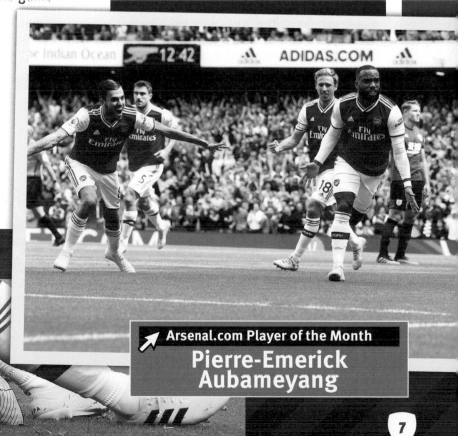

↖ **Arsenal.com Player of the Month**
Pierre-Emerick Aubameyang

SEPTEMBER

The month kicked off with a dramatic north London derby, in which we fought back from 2-0 down in the first half to earn a point at Emirates Stadium. Lacazette crashed home our first goal just before half-time, and Aubameyang scored from Matteo Guendouzi's cross to level in the second half. There was another 2-2 draw in the next game - at Watford - but this time we were on the receiving end of a comeback, having led 2-0 through a first-half Aubameyang brace. Bukayo Saka made his first eye-catching performance of the season in our opening Europa League game. The 18-year-old claimed his first senior goal, either side of setting up Joe Willock and Aubameyang in a convincing display in Germany, against a side who had remained unbeaten in European competition at home for more than 10 years. The goals continued to flow in the next couple of games - a comeback win over Villa at home, and a comfortable Carabao Cup defeat of Nottingham Forest. Martinelli stole the show against Forest, scoring his first two goals for the club, while Kieran Tierney made his debut, and Hector Bellerin made a welcome comeback from injury. We finished the month with a draw at Old Trafford, thanks to Aubameyang's equaliser that was only awarded after the intervention of VAR.

RESULTS

Sun 1 Premier League **Tottenham Hotspur (H)**
2-2 *Lacazette, Aubameyang*

Sun 15 Premier League **Watford (A)**
2-2 *Aubameyang 2*

Thur 19 Europa League **Eintracht Frankfurt (A)**
3-0 *Willock, Saka, Aubameyang*

Sun 22 Premier League **Aston Villa (H)**
3-2 *Pepe, Chambers, Aubameyang*

Tue 24 Carabao Cup **Nottingham Forest (H)**
5-0 *Martinelli 2, Holding, Willock, Nelson*

Mon 30 Premier League **Manchester United (A)**
1-1 *Aubameyang*

Arsenal.com Player of the Month
Matteo Guendouzi

OCTOBER

RESULTS

RESULTS

Thur 3 Europa League
Standard Liege (H)
4-0 *Martinelli 2, Willock, Ceballos*

Sun 6 Premier League
Bournemouth (H)
1-0 *David Luiz*

Mon 21 Premier League
Sheffield United (A)
0-1

Thur 24 Europa League
Vitoria (H)
3-2 *Martinelli, Pepe 2*

Sun 27 Premier League
Crystal Palace (H)
2-2 *Sokratis, David Luiz*

Wed 30 Carabao Cup
Liverpool (A)
5-5 (lost on penalties)
Torreira, Martinelli 2, Maitland-Niles, Willock

Martinelli's profile continued to rise in October, and it started with a Europa League brace in the 4-0 win over Standard Liege - in which we were three goals to the good inside 22 minutes. Fellow Brazilian David Luiz claimed his first Gunners goal to earn us all three points at home to Bournemouth, but we fell to only our second defeat of the season after a lacklustre performance at Bramall Lane, dropping us to fifth in the table. We bounced back in our next game though, with Pepe stealing the show. We were trailing 2-1 with 10 minutes remaining before the Ivorian scored two fantastic direct free-kicks to maintain our 100 per cent record in Europe. There was further disappointment back in the Premier League however – after leading Crystal Palace 2-0 inside 10 minutes at home, the visitors hit back twice in the second half to take a point. Sokratis had a late goal ruled out by VAR to compound our anguish. The month finished with a 10-goal thriller at Anfield in the Carabao Cup. Willock's screamer was the pick of the goals, and it seemed to be sending us into the quarter-finals, but Liverpool struck an injury-time equaliser, then prevailed 5-4 on penalties, with Ceballos having his spot kick saved.

↗ **Arsenal.com Player of the Month**
Gabriel Martinelli

NOVEMBER

Unai Emery's reign came to an end after failing to win a match in the month of November – a 2-1 defeat to Eintracht Frankfurt proving the final straw. The team squandered more leads at the start of the month - at home to Wolves in the Premier League, then in Portugal in the Europa League. Our chances of reaching the top four suffered a huge blow with a 2-0 defeat at the King Power Stadium. After the international break we dropped more points at home to Southampton, but at least avoided defeat thanks to Lacazette's strike deep into injury-time. But after Eintracht Frankfurt came from behind to claim a Europa League group stage win at the Emirates, Emery's time as manager came to an end, after 78 games in charge. He was replaced on a temporary basis by assistant head coach Freddie Ljungberg.

RESULTS

Sat 2 Premier League
Wolves (H)
1-1 *Aubameyang*

Wed 6 Europa League
Vitoria (A)
1-1 *Mustafi*

Sat 9 Premier League
Leicester City (A)
0-2

Sat 23 Premier League
Southampton (H)
2-2 *Lacazette 2*

Thur 28 Europa League
Eintracht Frankfurt (H)
1-2 *Aubameyang*

Arsenal.com Player of the Month
Bernd Leno

DECEMBER

Freddie Ljungberg's first game as caretaker boss was away to Norwich City in the Premier League, but we could only muster a draw at Carrow Road, with Aubameyang twice netting equalisers. Defeat at home to Brighton in the next game made it nine matches without a win before the run came to an end away to West Ham. Martinelli scored his first Premier League goal to level the scores, then Pepe scored a cracker to put us ahead and Aubameyang sealed the win late on. We rallied from two goals down in Belgium to earn the point that secured qualification to the knock out stages of the Europa League, and Ljungberg oversaw two more Premier League games before Mikel Arteta was named as the new permanent head coach. Our former midfielder's first match in charge was on Boxing Day away to Bournemouth, and it was Aubameyang to the rescue again with a second-half equaliser. It looked as though we were on the way to all three points against Chelsea in the final match of 2019 once Aubameyang had fired us into the lead. But the visitors scored twice in the final seven minutes to condemn us to a painful defeat.

↗ **Arsenal.com Player of the Month**
Lucas Torreira

RESULTS

Sun 1 Premier League
Norwich City (A)
2-2 *Aubameyang 2*

Thur 5 Premier League
Brighton & HA (H)
1-2 *Lacazette*

Mon 9 Premier League
West Ham United (A)
3-1 *Martinelli, Pepe, Aubameyang*

Thur 12 Europa League
Standard Liege (A)
2-2 *Lacazette, Saka*

Sun 15 Premier League
Manchester City (H)
0-3

Sat 21 Premier League
Everton (A)
0-0

Thur 26 Premier League
Bournemouth (A)
1-1 *Aubameyang*

Sun 29 Premier League
Chelsea (H)
1-2 *Aubameyang*

JANUARY

The new year brought new hope, as we kicked off 2020 in fine style, with a magnificent 2-0 home win over Manchester United to give Arteta his first victory in charge. Pepe fired us in front inside 10 minutes and we were in control from that point onwards, with Sokratis adding a deserved second late in the first half. We followed up with victory in the FA Cup third round over Leeds United, in a game of hugely contrasting halves. The visitors dominated the opening 45 minutes, without finding the breakthrough, but we were a different side after the break, with Reiss Nelson's goal enough to send us through. Our progress in the league was checked by three consecutive draws. However the third of those, away to Chelsea, gave plenty of reason for optimism. Playing with 10 men since the 27th minute when David Luiz was sent off while also conceding a penalty, we twice came from behind to claim a point, with Martinelli's 70-yard run and cool finish the highlight of the game. Two more youngsters stole the show at the end of the month – Saka and Eddie Nketiah both claimed first-half goals as we booked our place in the fifth round of the FA Cup.

RESULTS

Wed 1 Premier League
Manchester United (H)
2-0 *Pepe, Sokratis*

Mon 6 FA Cup
Leeds United (H)
1-0 *Nelson*

Sat 11 Premier League
Crystal Palace (A)
1-1 *Aubameyang*

Sat 18 Premier League
Sheffield United (H)
1-1 *Martinelli*

Tue 21 Premier League
Chelsea (A)
2-2 *Martinelli, Bellerin*

Mon 27 FA Cup
Bournemouth (A)
2-1 *Saka, Nketiah*

> Arsenal.com Player of the Month
> # Gabriel Martinelli

FEBRUARY

Aubameyang returned from a three-game suspension in time for the trip to Burnley at the start of the month, but he was left frustrated as we played out the first goalless draw of the Arteta reign. The goals flowed in the next match though, after a less than inspiring first half. The talented frontline of Aubameyang, Pepe, Mesut Ozil and Lacazette were all on target in our biggest league win of the season. It was the perfect way to set up our return to European action, and our visit to the Greek capital for the first game of the knock out stages was a fruitful one, thanks to Lacazette's late winner. We made it three wins in the space of a week in a thrilling game at home to Everton. The visitors scored in the first and last minutes of the opening half, but in between those strikes, Nketiah and Aubameyang were also on target. Auba netted again seconds after the restart, and that was enough to take all three points, inching us up to ninth place,

and closing the gap to the top four. There was agony at the end of the month though - in the second leg of the Europa League round of 32. Olympiacos led 1-0 after 90 minutes to take us to extra-time, and just when it seemed Aubameyang's spectacular strike would send us through, the Greeks netted in the last minute to go through on away goals. Amazingly Aubameyang had a chance in injury time to grab a dramatic winner, but he stabbed wide from close range.

RESULTS

Sun 2 Premier League
Burnley (A)
0-0

Sun 16 Premier League
Newcastle Unite (H)
4-0 *Aubameyang, Pepe, Ozil, Lacazette*

Thur 20 Europa League
Olympiacos (A)
1-0 *Lacazette*

Sun 23 Premier League
Everton (H)
3-2 *Nketiah, Aubameyang 2*

Thur 27 Europa League
Olympiacos (H)
1-2 *Aubameyang*

MARCH

We regrouped for the FA Cup fifth round tie away to Portsmouth, and were too strong for the League One side. Defender Sokratis put us ahead just before the break, before Nketiah maintained his good form with the second to send us through to the quarter-finals. The only disappointment on the night was the ankle injury suffered by Torreira, causing him to be stretchered off. We kept another clean sheet the following weekend against struggling West Ham, with Lacazette's late goal - only given after the intervention of VAR - proving enough for the three points. Then the football stopped. Our next game was due to be away to Manchester City on March 11, but it was postponed as several of our players needed to self-isolate after coming into contact with Olympiacos owner Evangelos Marinakis, who had contracted COVID-19. Shortly afterwards Arteta himself tested positive with coronavirus, and soon all football in England was placed on hold indefinitely. We were sitting ninth in the table at the time, with 10 games still to play. We were the only unbeaten side in the Premier League in the calendar year.

RESULTS

Mon 2 FA Cup
Portsmouth (A)
2-0 *Sokratis, Nketiah*

Sat 7 Premier League
West Ham United (H)
1-0 *Lacazette*

JUNE

RESULTS

Wed 17 Premier League
Manchester City (A)
0-3

Sat 20 Premier League
Brighton & Hove Albion (A)
1-2 *Pepe*

Thur 25 Premier League
Southampton (A)
2-0 *Nketiah, Willock*

Sun 28 FA Cup
Sheffield United (A)
2-1 *Pepe, Ceballos*

Finally, after 102 days without action, we were back in business - but it was unlike anything we had ever seen before. Our first game back was against reigning champions Manchester City, played behind closed doors, making for an unusually eerie atmosphere. After suffering two injuries in the opening half hour, we conceded either side of the break, then lost David Luiz to a red card, before the hosts sealed the points in injury-time. There was more frustration – and more injury problems – in the next game at Brighton. After Bernd Leno was stretchered off in the first half, Pepe gave us the lead with a stunner, but the hosts struck back with two goals in the final 15 minutes to leave us empty-handed. However, our fortunes changed a few days later, in another away game on the south coast. Nketiah gave us the lead in the first half against Southampton before fellow academy product Willock sealed the much-needed points late on. The month finished on a high after late drama in the FA Cup quarter-final. Pepe slotted home a penalty to give us the lead, only for hosts Sheffield United to equalise late on. But we had the final say in injury time, thanks to a very smart finish from Ceballos - sending us to Wembley yet again!

▶ **Arsenal.com Player of the Month**
Kieran Tierney

15

JULY

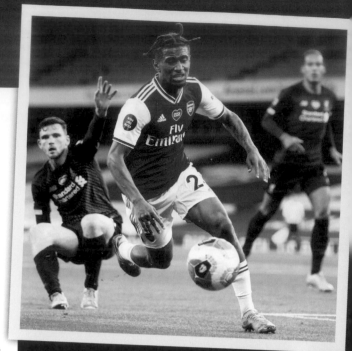

The winning run continued into July, with a thumping victory over Norwich City in our first ever behind-closed-doors match at the Emirates. Aubameyang netted twice - including his 50th Premier League goal, reaching the landmark quicker than any player in the club's history. Cedric Soares came on to make his debut late on, and marked the occasion with a left-footed cracker. Saka celebrated signing a new contract with the club by scoring his first Premier League goal in the win at Wolves. We looked to be on course for five successive wins after another Aubameyang goal at home to Leicester, but conceded a late equaliser after being reduced to ten men following Nketiah's sending off. We again conceded late on to lose the first north London derby at the new Tottenham Hotspur Stadium, but bounced back in spectacular style. First, we came from behind to beat newly crowned-champions Liverpool 2-1 at the Emirates – Nelson's first Premier League goal proved to be the winner. Then, just three days later, we humbled holders Manchester City in the FA Cup semi-final, thanks to a magnificent brace from Aubameyang and a determined and resilient defensive display at Wembley. We finished eighth in the table after taking three points from our last two games, beating Watford 3-2 at home on the final day thanks to another double from Aubameyang - taking him to 22 Premier League goals for the campaign - and Tierney's first goal for the club.

RESULTS

Wed 1 Premier League
Norwich City (H)
4-0 *Aubameyang 2, Xhaka, Cedric*

Sat 4 Premier League
Wolves (A)
2-0 *Saka, Lacazette*

Tue 7 Premier League
Leicester City (H)
1-1 *Aubameyang*

Sun 12 Premier League
Tottenham Hotspur (A)
1-2 *Lacazette*

Wed 15 Premier League
Liverpool (H)
2-1 *Lacazette, Nelson*

Sat 18 FA Cup
Manchester City (N)
2-0 *Aubameyang 2*

Tue 21 Premier League
Aston Villa (A)
0-1

Sun 26 Premier League
Watford (H)
3-2 *Aubameyang 2, Tierney*

↗ **Arsenal.com Player of the Season**
Pierre-Emerick Aubameyang

AUGUST

So, it all came down to the last match of an incredible, marathon season, that started in August 2019 and finished in August 2020. A win would see us qualify for Europe, as well as lift the famous trophy for a record-extending 14th time.

RESULT

Sat 1 FA Cup
Chelsea (N) 2-1 *Aubameyang 2*

Turn the page to relive an unforgettable day at Wembley.

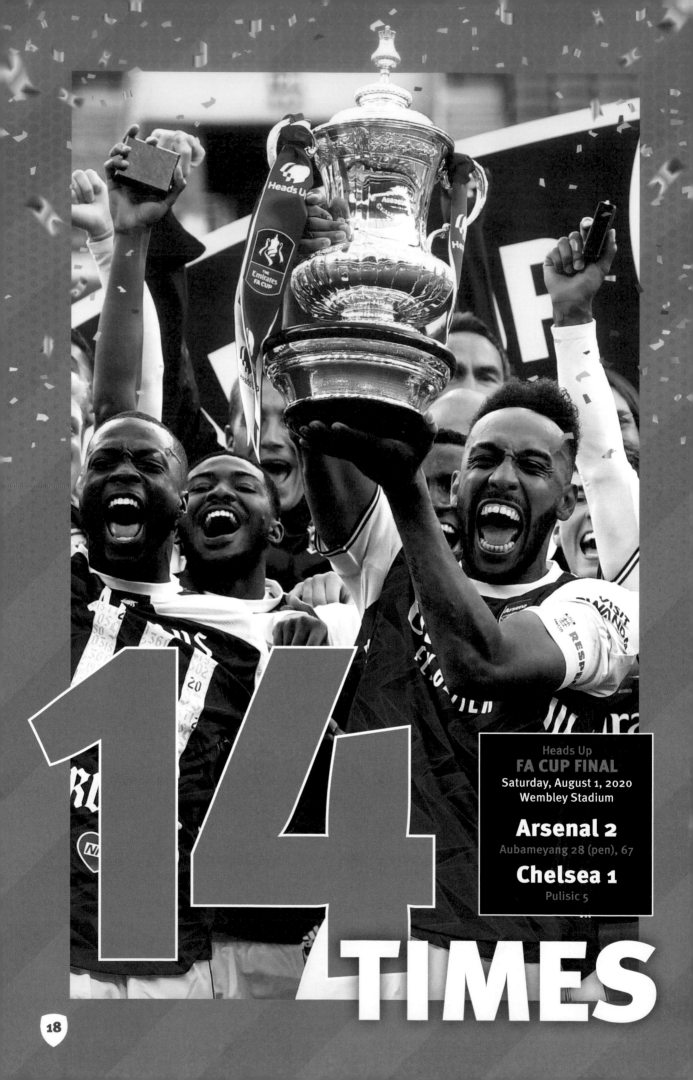

14 TIMES

Heads Up
FA CUP FINAL
Saturday, August 1, 2020
Wembley Stadium

Arsenal 2
Aubameyang 28 (pen), 67

Chelsea 1
Pulisic 5

We extended our record as the most successful club in the history of the FA Cup when we beat Chelsea 2-1 behind-closed-doors in the 2020 'Lockdown Final'. Top scorer and captain Pierre-Emerick Aubameyang scored twice to seal our 14th FA Cup triumph, earning Mikel Arteta his first major honour in just his 28th game as head coach.

We had to fight back from behind to win it too. Chelsea's Christian Pulisic scored the opening goal within five minutes, but we soon composed ourselves to take control of the game. Nicolas Pepe netted an absolute screamer, but the offside flag was already up. Moments later Aubameyang raced through into the area, where he was hauled down by Cesar Azpilicueta. Referee Anthony Taylor pointed to the penalty spot, and Auba himself struck home firmly into the side netting to level the game.

The striker grabbed the winner in the second half, with a typically classy finish. Hector Bellerin started the move with a dynamic run from his own half, before Pepe fed the ball to Aubameyang just inside the area. From there Auba skipped past Kurt Zouma before dinking his finish over goalkeeper Willy Caballero left footed. Chelsea later had Mateo Kovacic sent off for a second bookable offence and we comfortably saw out the win to kick start the celebrations in an empty Wembley Stadium.

ARSENAL LINE-UP

Martinez, Bellerin, Holding, David Luiz (Sokratis 88), Tierney (Kolasinac 90), Ceballos, Xhaka, Maitland-Niles, Pepe, Lacazette (Nketiah 82), Aubameyang.

Subs not used: Torreira, Nelson, Willock, Saka, Smith, Macey.

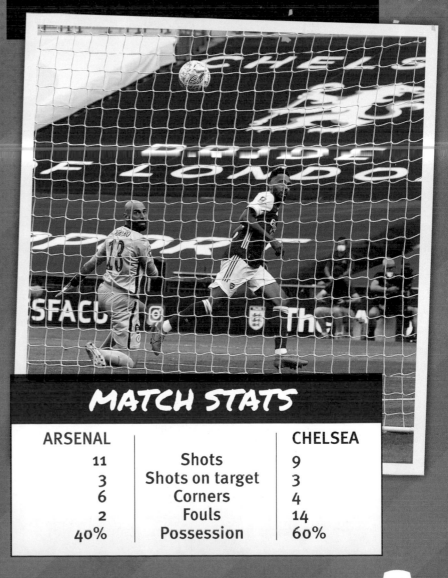

MATCH STATS

ARSENAL		CHELSEA
11	Shots	9
3	Shots on target	3
6	Corners	4
2	Fouls	14
40%	Possession	60%

MATCH FACTS

• This was our 14th win in the competition and a record 21st appearance in the final.

• We have won each of our past seven appearances in the FA Cup final.

• Mikel Arteta is only the second person to win the FA Cup for us as both player and manager, following George Graham.

• At 31 years and 44 days, Pierre-Emerick Aubameyang is our second oldest goalscorer in an FA Cup final, after Bob John against Newcastle in 1932.

• Only six players have ever scored more than once in FA Cup finals for us: Reg Lewis, Ian Wright, Freddie Ljungberg, Aaron Ramsey, Alexis Sanchez and Pierre-Emerick Aubameyang.

• This was the 10th time we have won the cup wearing red and white, compared to four in yellow and blue.

OUR 14 WINS

Season	Opposition	Score	Scorers	Venue
1929/30	Huddersfield Town	2-0	James, Lambert	Wembley Stadium
1935/36	Sheffield United	1-0	Drake	Wembley Stadium
1949/50	Liverpool	2-0	Lewis 2	Wembley Stadium
1970/71	Liverpool	2-1	Kelly, George	Wembley Stadium
1978/79	Manchester United	3-2	Talbot, Stapleton, Sunderland	Wembley Stadium
1992/93	Sheffield Wednesday	1-1	Wright	Wembley Stadium
1992/93 (replay)	Sheffield Wednesday	2-1	Wright, Linighan	Wembley Stadium
1997/98	Newcastle United	2-0	Overmars, Anelka	Wembley Stadium
2001/02	Chelsea	2-0	Parlour, Ljungberg	Millennium Stadium
2002/03	Southampton	1-0	Pires	Millennium Stadium
2004/05	Manchester United	0-0*	(won 5-4 on penalties)	Millennium Stadium
2013/14	Hull City	3-2	Cazorla, Koscielny, Ramsey	Wembley Stadium
2014/15	Aston Villa	4-0	Walcott, Alexis, Mertesacker, Giroud	Wembley Stadium
2016/17	Chelsea	2-1	Alexis, Ramsey	Wembley Stadium
2019/20	Chelsea	2-1	Aubameyang 2	Wembley Stadium

MOST FA CUP WINS

Arsenal	14
Manchester United	12
Chelsea	8
Tottenham Hotspur	8
Liverpool	7
Aston Villa	7

MOST FA CUP FINALS

Arsenal	21
Manchester United	20
Chelsea	14
Liverpool	14
Newcastle United	13

ARSENAL'S FA CUP WINNING MANAGERS

Arsène Wenger	7
George Allison	1
Mikel Arteta	1
Herbert Chapman	1
George Graham	1
Bertie Mee	1
Terry Neill	1
Tom Whittaker	1

FAMILY LIFE

What did our players get up to with their families when they were younger?

FAMILY MEALS

 Pablo Mari: "In Valencia, paella is the classic thing you eat on a Sunday when the family gets together. The ingredients of the perfect Valencia paella are a family secret!"

 Bukayo Saka: "My favourite meal was my mum's plantain, it's so good."

Rob Holding: "We all sat round the table, no phones allowed, that was my dad's rule. Me, my sister and my mum and dad would all sit round and chat while we ate, and on Sundays we would usually have a roast dinner."

Sokratis: "Every Saturday we would get together with the whole family, cousins, grandparents, sitting outside and we would have a big lunch. My mum would cook for everyone, and she is a very good cook. It would be traditional Greek food, olives and all the usual."

GAMES

Pablo Mari: "We used to play cards, dominoes, parchis. The whole family spent many Sunday afternoons playing parchis for hours after we'd had our paella."

Reiss Nelson: "I loved playing table tennis. My sister worked at an adventure playground, where the kids used to go after school, and you could play table tennis there, or pool, stuff like that, and I loved table tennis there after school."

 **Calum Chambers:** "We went through a stage of playing Monopoly but it got too long and too competitive!"

 Alexandre Lacazette: We played dominoes because it's really popular within my family, and with people from the Caribbean. We used to play cards as well, but to be honest I never understood the rules so I much preferred to play dominoes."

HOLIDAYS

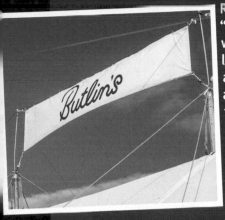

Reiss Nelson: "We mostly went to resorts like Butlin's and Haven, and I enjoyed those a lot. I used to love going on the arcades, going swimming, stuff like that."

Bernd Leno: "We went to many places in Europe – Spain, Italy looking for a sandy beach. We also went to Russia - both of my parents are from there, and my brother was born there too. I'm the only one in my family born in Germany."

Shkodran Mustafi: The only holidays we had during the six-week break from school in the summer were always to Albania. That was the only destination, for the whole of the six weeks. Never anywhere else. We used to go by bus – it took 28 hours at least. If there was traffic, or problems at the border, it could take 35 hours. But honestly, I loved it."

Kieran Tierney: "Every summer we would go away, somewhere like Spain. We went to Mallorca a few times and sometimes in Easter we would maybe go away in a caravan or something like that."

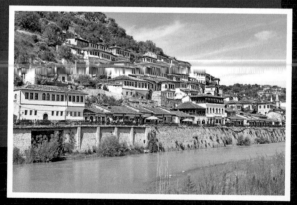

PETS

Reiss Nelson: "When I was five my brother got a dog called Lady, which was with us all the way until quite recently when it died. We were very upset because she was part of the family."

Pablo Mari: "When I was young I'd find dogs on the street and bring them home. The first one was called Thor. Then we had a little female dog that I called Nala."

Rob Holding: "We had a rabbit when I was really young. It was called Todd, though I've no idea why, I was very young. We always wanted a dog but we were never allowed."

Nicolas Pepe: "When I was small, together with my sister I had a rabbit, a hamster and a dog."

23

PLAYER SPOTLIGHT

3
DEF

KIERAN TIERNEY

BORN: DOUGLAS, ISLE OF MAN, JUNE 5, 1997
NATIONALITY: SCOTTISH
JOINED ARSENAL: FROM CELTIC ON AUGUST 8, 2019
PREVIOUS CLUB: CELTIC
ARSENAL DEBUT: V NOTTINGHAM FOREST (H), LEAGUE CUP, SEPTEMBER 24, 2019

A summer signing in 2019, Scotland international left back Kieran finally made his debut after recovering from injury in a 5-0 home win over Nottingham Forest at Emirates Stadium in September 2019. Blessed with an excellent work ethic, he then proceeded to show the talent that had made him such hot property in Scottish football with stunning assists against Standard Liege and Vitoria in the Europa League, before again starring after the lockdown, in either central defence or at wing back. Prior to joining the Gunners tough-tackling Kieran had spent his whole career with Celtic, where he won four consecutive league titles, and was named PFA Scotland Young Player of the Year three times.

PLAYER SPOTLIGHT

4
DEF

WILLIAM SALIBA

BORN: BONDY, FRANCE, MARCH 24, 2001
NATIONALITY: FRENCH
JOINED ARSENAL: FROM ST ETIENNE ON JULY 25, 2019
PREVIOUS CLUB: ST ETIENNE

Having signed during the summer of 2019, promising young defender William spent the whole of last season back on loan at previous club St Etienne. The powerful yet elegant centre back has quickly built a reputation as one of the hottest prospects on the continent, after bursting on to the scene in 2018/19. A France youth international at every level from under-16 to under-20, William was coached by Kylian Mbappe's father in his tender years. Of Cameroonian descent, he enjoyed another fine season in Ligue 1 last term, helping his side reach the final of the French Cup, although injury ruled him out of action for three months during the winter.

WHO'S OLDER?

Who is older out of the following pairs of players?

1. Ian Wright or David Seaman?

2. Freddie Ljungberg or Dennis Bergkamp?

3. Thierry Henry or Robert Pires?

4. Cesc Fabregas or Jack Wilshere?

5. Pierre-Emerick Aubameyang or Theo Walcott?

6. Mikel Arteta or Tomas Rosicky?

7. Bukayo Saka or Gabriel Martinelli?

8. Joe Willock or Kieran Tierney?

9. Reiss Nelson or Rob Holding?

10. Bernd Leno or Emi Martinez?

26

Answers on page 61

FACE SWAP

We've got some seriously mixed up players here! But can you tell who they are?

A

B

C

Answers on page 61

WORKING FROM HOME

During lockdown many of our players took to Instagram to show how they were managing to keep up their training regime, or spending the time with their family. Here are some of their posts...

Emiliano Martinez @Emi_martinez26

The work continues 💪🏻
#emi #arsenal #stayathome

Hector Bellerin @hectorbellerin

Quarantine garden fits

Gabriel Martinelli @ga_martinelli1

Focus 😛💪🏻 #stayathome

Mesut Ozil @m10_official

Hanging out with my lovely dogs
☀️🖤 #Balboa #Pablito #PostWorkout
🚴🏻💦 #Hometeam #StayAtHome 🏠 #M1Ö

David Luiz @davidluiz_4

Done 💪

Bernd Leno @berndleno1

Happy Easter 🐣 🐰

Shkodran Mustafi @shkodranmustafi

Had a weak moment and went out with my new ride for some ice cream 🍦 Got caught right away. So I will wait for real ice cream until iftar 🙌 #SM20

Lucas Torreira @ltorreira34

I'm back #LT11 ⚽🖤 #Gunners

MAGIC MOMENTS

We asked the players to recall one game that was special from their career to date...

Manchester United 1-1 Arsenal
Date: September 30, 2019 Venue: Old Trafford

BUKAYO SAKA

Bukayo says: "The game for me was playing at Old Trafford last season. I had been there before as a fan, but now I was here as a player. My dad took me to watch Manchester United v Newcastle, in the Newcastle end, because he's a Newcastle fan, and I liked Man United back then. It was a big moment for me to be in the stadium because I didn't go to many games as a kid. I was about eight or nine at the time. So when I got to play there, being down on the pitch, looking up at the fans in the stand, that's when it hit me. It's a huge stadium too, of course, that's when I really realised what was starting to happen. My dad is still the one who gets into me most after games, even if I've done well, scored a goal or whatever, he will be there telling me what I need to do to improve. But my whole family support me really well, my uncles always pray for me, check up on me and always want to know how I am getting on. It's really nice to have that. After the Bournemouth game when I was man of the match, my mum was the first to text me, just telling me how proud she was."

NICOLAS PEPE

Nico says: "Probably the match I played for Lille at Toulouse where we won 3-2 to avoid relegation from Ligue 1. I scored two important goals and my dad was delighted that day. There was also another match at Marseille where we won 3-1 and I got two goals. That was such a special occasion for my dad. He watched me play at his beloved Stade Velodrome and I scored twice."

Toulouse 2-3 Lille
Date: May 6, 2018 Venue: Stadium Municipal

ROB HOLDING

Rob says: "Definitely the FA Cup semi-final in 2017 against Man City. I had a lot of old schoolmates there as well - all City fans - and they were in the away end that day. My grandad was there too and I remember him crying after the game. He said to me that he could die a happy man, because he saw his grandson win a cup semi-final at Wembley. He was at the final as well, which was also special, and it helped that I played pretty well."

Arsenal 2-1 Manchester City
Date: April 23, 2017 Venue: Wembley Stadium

SHKODRAN MUSTAFI

Anderlecht 1-2 Arsenal
Date: October 22, 2014
Venue: Lotto Stadium

Sampdoria 1-0 Atalanta
Date: October 26, 2013
Venue: Luigi Ferraris Stadium

Shkodran says: "For me a special game was when I scored my first goal for Sampdoria, because my cousins and family were all there. I think 10 of them came over. They just decided the night before so they called me and said they were on their way, driving through Switzerland and then into Italy. They came and they were in the stadium to see me score my first goal as a professional. I think it was the winning goal as well, so it's a very special memory for me."

EMILIANO MARTINEZ

Emi says: "A game that meant a lot to me was my debut in the Champions League against Anderlecht in 2014. My dad travelled for 21 hours to watch that game. I found out two days beforehand that I would be playing, so I called my dad and told him the news. He said he would definitely be there. So he got a bus for six and a half hours to the airport, then flew for 13 hours to London, then took another flight to get to Belgium, and then from the airport to the stadium on another bus. He got there just in time for the game, and we won as well with two late goals. He was crying afterwards and telling me how proud of me he was."

31

EMILE SMITH ROWE

Emile says: "Obviously my first team debut in the Europa League was very special. It's something I had dreamt of, and my family were all there to see it. That was a very big moment but I have to say that when I scored at the Emirates against Blackpool, that was the craziest feeling ever. Everyone was there again to see it and to be honest I hadn't even thought about scoring, so when it happened I wasn't ready for it - just going crazy."

Arsenal 4-2 Vorskla Poltava
Date: September 20, 2018 Venue: Emirates Stadium

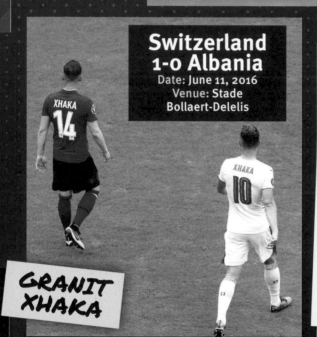

Switzerland 1-0 Albania
Date: June 11, 2016
Venue: Stade Bollaert-Delelis

BERND LENO

GRANIT XHAKA

Chelsea 2-0 Bayer Leverkusen
Date: September 13, 2011
Venue: Stamford Bridge

Granit says: "My parents were both there watching me against my brother Taulant when we played at Euro 2016. My mother had a half-and-half Switzerland and Albania shirt! It's a very special memory, and if I speak about it with them today, they start to get very emotional. It was not so easy for them to see their children against each other. My brother plays the same position, so we were in direct opposition. Everybody knew we were brothers, and my parents told us before the game. "Respect each other, play your game. Go to your maximum, your limits, but respect each other. I don't want to see anything bad between you both!" She said that because she knows we are so competitive! We enjoyed it, but it wasn't easy for us. To be honest it was hardest before the game, but when it started, you don't think about it so much, and you are just focussed on the game. That's all you think about. So we enjoyed it, but I don't want to play against him again! I know my parents were very proud though afterwards – it's not every day you have your two sons playing against each other in such a big stadium and occasion. It was crazy."

Bernd says: "I remember my first Champions League game at Stamford Bridge when I was 19. I was playing for Bayer Leverkusen at the time. Of course, my first Bundesliga game was special as well but this was just a month later, and my parents came to London to watch it. They don't speak English but they wanted to come and watch me in the Champions League. They were confident they could do it even without speaking English. They showed the taxi driver a picture of the stadium and they made it there. I played a very good game and at the end our fans were screaming my name so when I saw my parents afterwards they were very proud. I was still very young. I had been playing for Stuttgart Under-23s and then moved to Leverkusen, and a month before this game I had played in front of 1,000 people, then just a month later I was playing in front of a huge crowd at Stamford Bridge. It was a dream for me and my parents."

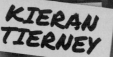

KIERAN TIERNEY

Celtic 2-0 Ross County
Date: August 1, 2016
Venue: Celtic Park

Kieran says: "Every single home game for Celtic, I would be on the pitch and wave up to my family in the stands, then turn and wave some more to someone else, then turn again and wave at a different group. I was stood out on the pitch waving to people for five minutes! 'Have I forgotten anyone? Oh yeah, there's some in the top tier too, I'll wave up there.' It was quite funny, but I could pinpoint exactly where they were in the stadium, because they had been in the same positions for years. But, yeah, my debut was pretty special. I had played a couple of friendlies, which were brilliant, but the competitive debut was the best. I only came on for 10 minutes, we were away at Dundee but my family were all there that day. The next season my home debut was on Flag Day. We had won the league the season before, so the first home game of the season the fans brought their flags and it was great. The other left back was suspended so I played, and I know my mum and dad were really, really proud that day, to see me play at Celtic Park in front of 60,000."

Brazil 3-0 Spain
Date: June 30, 2013 Venue: Maracana Stadium

David says: "There have been many games that were special because my family were there. I always say that everything I do is for one purpose: to make my family happy. I am always thankful for what they did for me in my life. They sacrificed their own dreams for me. I even my sister as well. They all came to support me when I was starting out. My mum loved football as well, and played it a bit. It's as if everything they did was to help me, so now I just want to thank them. I think a particularly memorable game for me was for Brazil in the final of the Confederations Cup in 2013. We won the game, I saved the ball on the line, and the whole Maracana was singing my name. My family were all there, in fact with friends and family I had more than 100 people there that day in the Maracana. Afterwards my friends told me that my mum was crying and my dad was too when the crowd sang my name. It was a special game. Afterwards I gave my shirt to my parents. In fact, I remember just after I became professional for Vitoria in Brazil, I got home during one of my holidays and my mum and dad invited me to their room. They showed me the first ever pair of football boots that I had worn. They had kept all of my boots from when I was six years old, and I had no idea. I didn't know about it so I said, 'Why did you keep these?' and my dad turned to me and said, 'Because I knew you were going to make it. I knew you would be a footballer one day.'"

DAVID LUIZ

PLAYER SPOTLIGHT

7
FWD

BUKAYO SAKA

BORN: EALING, SEPTEMBER 5, 2001
NATIONALITY: ENGLISH
JOINED ARSENAL: AS A SCHOLAR IN SUMMER 2018
PREVIOUS CLUBS: NONE
ARSENAL DEBUT: V VORSKLA POLTAVA (A) EUROPA LEAGUE, NOVEMBER 29, 2018

Talented youngster Bukayo burst onto the scene in stunning fashion last term, establishing himself as one of the first names on Mikel Arteta's team sheet by the end of the season. Having broken into the side at left back, the pacy, skilful academy product - who has been at the club from the age of seven - soon began to show his creative skills as he racked up the assists. His first senior goal came in the 3-0 win over Eintracht Frankfurt in September, and he never looked back, ending 2019/20 with 12 assists and four goals from 38 appearances.

PLAYER SPOTLIGHT

12
FWD

WILLIAN

BORN: RIBEIRAO PIRES, BRAZIL, AUGUST 9, 1988
NATIONALITY: BRAZILIAN
JOINED ARSENAL: FROM CHELSEA ON AUGUST 14, 2020
PREVIOUS CLUBS: CORINTHIANS, SHAKHTAR DONETSK, ANZHI MAKHACHKALA, CHELSEA

Experienced Brazil international Willian swapped west London for north London when he joined us in pre-season after a seven-year career with Chelsea. The exciting winger - who is comfortable on both flanks - won five trophies, including two league titles with his previous club, and also won four league titles while with Shakhtar Donetsk in Ukraine. A long-standing member of the Brazil international setup, he won the Copa America in 2019 and also played in two World Cups. Fast, skilful and with a willingness to carry out his defensive duties, Willian has been a star performer in the Premier League over the past few years – impressing with his quick feet, exceptional technical level and quality from set pieces.

SPOT THE DIFFERENCE

Can you spot the eight differences between these two pictures?

Answers on page 61

TRUE OR FALSE

Can you work out which of the following 10 statements are true, and which we have made up?

1. Bernd Leno was born in Russia.

2. Mikel Arteta's wife was named Miss Spain in 1999.

3. Nicolas Pepe won a Ferrari in a lottery when he was 18.

4. Kieran Tierney won a major trophy once every 21 games on average in his Celtic career.

5. Rob Holding played professional rugby for two seasons before taking up football.

6. Reiss Nelson has played under four different Arsenal managers.

7. Pablo Mari once grew 12 centimetres taller in just one summer.

8. David Luiz is the only player to have won the World Cup, Champions League, Premier League and FA Cup.

9. Bukayo Saka is a qualified mechanic.

10. Gabriel Martinelli had trials at Manchester United before joining Arsenal.

Answers on page 61

OZIL

MARTINELLI

BELLERIN

Get creative and get those pens out - it's time to design some new kits for the Arsenal stars!

TORREIRA

PEPE

19

ARSENAL WOMEN

After the 2019/20 domestic season was cut short due to the global pandemic, Arsenal Women boss Joe Montemurro set about reshaping his squad for the next campaign.

As defending champions, Arsenal were third in the Women's Super League table when the decision was made to bring a premature end to the league season in May. But the break in play didn't mean it was a quiet time for the club.

Montemurro pulled off some particularly eye-catching new signings as the side attempts to reclaim the league title in 2020/21.

Here's the lowdown on the new faces at the club.

NOELLE MARITZ
Position: Defender
Born: California, USA, December 23, 1995
Signed from: Wolfsburg

Although born in America, Noelle is an established Switzerland international, having grown up in the country and thus acquiring dual-nationality. She has already amassed nearly 100 international caps, despite still being in her mid-20s, after making her Switzerland debut in 2013, aged just 17. Versatile Noelle can play anywhere in defence, but also likes to get forward: "Yes, I'm a defender and I love to get involved with tackling, duels and winning the ball back," she said. "But I also love to be up front sometimes! I'm calm on the ball and I like to play possession football, but I really enjoy the offensive part too. "Noelle won five Bundesliga titles with Wolfsburg, as well as six German cups and the Champions League title in 2014.

MALIN GUT
Position: Midfielder
Born: Lenzburg, Switzerland,
August 1, 2000
Signed from: Grasshopper

Young midfielder Malin is an international teammate of fellow Gunners Lia Walti and Noelle Maritz in the Switzerland national team - and is a similar type of player to Lia. A ball-playing, defensive midfielder, Malin has bags of potential and also contributed some valuable goals for former clubs Grasshopper and FC Zurich in her home country. "It's a very big honour for me to be able to play and represent this club in the future," Malin said. "From the beginning it felt like everything fitted perfectly. I talked to Joe a lot which helped because he was really able to convince me from the first second and I felt that he's the kind of coach I really want to play with. I'm very, very excited to play with the Arsenal shirt for the first time."

Vastly experienced goalkeeper Lydia joins from Melbourne City, where current Gunners boss Joe Montemurro had managed her previously. A long-standing Australia international since 2005, Lydia has enjoyed a hugely successful club career as well, both in her home country and for several sides in America, and also in Sweden. Twice voted Australian player of the year, she is widely regarded as one of the best keepers in the nation's history, and is an excellent shot stopper as well as being a commanding presence inside the area. "I remember watching Arsenal as a young kid, it was like the only football to watch back in Australia, so it's amazing to be a part of the team," she said. Lydia has a fascinating back story too - in fact she has written a children's book 'Saved' about her unconventional childhood growing up in the desert with her Aboriginal father and American mother. She is also a qualified zookeeper!

LYDIA WILLIAMS
Position: Goalkeeper
Born: Katanning, Australia,
May 13, 1988
Signed from: Melbourne City

STEPH CATLEY
Position: Defender
Born: Melbourne, Australia,
January 26, 1994
Signed from: Reign FC

Left-back Steph is widely acknowledged as being one of the best players in her position in world football. Steph started her career at Melbourne Victory and since went on to play for Portland Thorns FC, Orlando Pride and OL Reign of Washington. Vice-captain of the Australia team, she is closing in on a century of appearances for her country, after making her debut aged 18. An attack-minded full-back, she won the W-League Championship five times and W-League Premiership twice, in addition to being named W-League Young Player of the Year and FFA U-20 Footballer of the Year twice. "This is something that I've been looking forward to for a long time," she said. "Arsenal is a place where I've imagined myself playing for a long time too. This will be my first taste of European football and obviously there's so much to look forward to and so many big occasions to come. I can't wait to get started."

PLAYER SPOTLIGHT

14
FWD

PIERRE-EMERICK AUBAMEYANG

BORN: LAVAL, FRANCE, JUNE 18, 1989
NATIONALITY: GABONESE
JOINED ARSENAL: FROM BORUSSIA DORTMUND ON JANUARY 31, 2018
PREVIOUS CLUBS: AC MILAN, DIJON (LOAN), LILLE (LOAN), MONACO (LOAN), SAINT-ETIENNE, BORUSSIA DORTMUND
ARSENAL DEBUT: V EVERTON (H) LEAGUE, FEBRUARY 3, 2018

Prolific marksman Auba led our scoring charts again in 2019/20, excelling after taking the captaincy in November 2019. The explosive striker netted 29 times in all competitions, including a brace in the FA Cup final win over Chelsea at Wembley, to take his club tally to 70 goals. His return was even more impressive considering he often played on the left wing in a three-man attack. The Premier League Golden Boot winner in 2018/19, the Gabon international narrowly missed out on that honour again last term, but is widely regarded as one of the world's leading strikers. He had previously proved himself as a natural goalscorer at German side Borussia Dortmund, where he scored 141 times in five seasons.

PLAYER SPOTLIGHT

17
DEF

CEDRIC SOARES

BORN: SINGEN, GERMANY, AUGUST 31, 1991
NATIONALITY: PORTUGUESE
JOINED ARSENAL: FROM SOUTHAMPTON ON JANUARY 31, 2020
PREVIOUS CLUBS: SPORTING, ACADEMICA (LOAN), SOUTHAMPTON, INTER MILAN (LOAN)
ARSENAL DEBUT: V NORWICH (H) LEAGUE, JULY 1, 2020

Initially signed on loan, Cedric had to wait until after the restart to make his debut, and he marked the occasion with a stunning left-foot strike in the 4-0 home win over Norwich in July. The right back joined on a short-term loan in the January transfer window, and the move was made permanent shortly before he made his debut. The versatile defender has plenty of experience of the Premier League, having spent four and a half years with Southampton before becoming a Gunner. He started his career at Sporting Lisbon, but also represented Inter Milan during a short loan spell. Although German-born, Cedric was raised in Lisbon and has represented Portugal at every level from under-16 to the senior team, and was part of the Euro 2016 winning side.

ARSENAL IN LOCKDOWN

Football had never known anything like it. Late on the evening of March 10 Arsenal's Premier League match with Manchester City - scheduled for the following day - was postponed. The decision was made as several of our players had come into contact with Olympiacos owner Evangelos Marinakis – who had tested positive for COVID-19 – when we played the Greek side two weeks earlier.

Two days later, on March 12, Arsenal closed the training ground after head coach Mikel Arteta himself tested positive for COVID-19. Soon afterwards all Premier League football was halted indefinitely, and the rest of the continent soon followed suit.

There followed a period of more than three months without football. At one stage it wasn't clear whether the Premier League season would be completed at all - with the Gunners sitting in ninth place with 10 matches remaining.

But gradually things returned to something like normal. At first the club's primary focus was on helping the huge effort in the local community, while the players took a voluntary pay cut and trained from home.

Training in small groups - while observing the social distancing rules - returned to London Colney, followed by behind-closed-doors friendlies at Emirates Stadium before the Premier League could resume - also behind closed doors - with that fixture away to Manchester City on June 17.

Here's a taste of what happened at Arsenal while the football stopped.

ARSENAL IN THE COMMUNITY

On March 25 volunteers from our community department prepared club cars that were donated to support and transport frontline NHS staff during the pandemic.

On April 17 defender Shkodran Mustafi marked his birthday by personally donating 16,000 meals to the Islington community.

MUSTI MAGIC

IN IT TOGETHER!

On April 10 the Arsenal Foundation joined forces with HIS Church to deliver 15 tonnes of emergency supplies into Islington. It was part of the club's wider response to the crisis – the Arsenal Foundation also pledged £100k to local organisations and redirected a further £50k of partnership funding with Islington Giving towards their COVID-19 Crisis Fund.

Throughout April and May Arsenal and the local community continued to show support for the amazing work of NHS staff and key workers during the pandemic.

THANK YOU NHS!

While much of the country was advised to work from home, many of our groundstaff were still needed to make sure Emirates Stadium would be ready for when the action resumed.

WORKING FROM HOME (OF FOOTBALL)

Given the go-ahead by the government and Premier League, we made some tentative steps back into training in late May, starting with non-contact, socially distanced sessions, all under the watchful eye of Mikel Arteta.

STOP
STOP + LOOK
RESPECT 2M RULE
FOR PEOPLE WALKING OTHER WAY

SOCIALLY DISTANCED TRAINING

The Premier League confirmed matches would resume on June 17, with our trip to Manchester City as one of the first games to be played upon resumption. So training stepped up a level, with full contact now permitted.

As the preparations ramped up, we organised some behind-closed-doors friendlies at the Emirates, to help get used to the feeling of playing inside an empty stadium. The first of those was against Charlton on June 6, with Eddie Nketiah scoring a hat-trick in a 3-0 win.

PROJECT RESTART

THE GREAT BIG ARSENAL QUIZ

40 big questions on all aspects of the Gunners!

1. Who are the only two players to score for us in the Premier League whose surname doesn't contain any letters from the word Arsenal?

2. What do the letters VCC stand for in Arsenal's motto?

3. At which stadium did we clinch the 2002 Premier League title?

4. Against which team did Dennis Bergkamp and Thierry Henry both score their first Arsenal goals?

5. We have won the FA Cup more than any other side, but how many times?

6. What year did Emirates Stadium open?

7. Which player scored in both the 2001 and 2002 FA Cup finals?

8. What squad number did Robert Pires, Nelson Vivas, David Platt and Tomas Rosicky all have in common?

9. Who were our shirt sponsors during the Invincible season?

10. What score did we beat Chelsea in the 2017 FA Cup final?

11. Against which team was Mikel Arteta's first game as head coach?

12. In what year were Arsenal founded?

13. Who is the youngest first-team player in our history?

14. What is the surname of Gavin and Justin – two brothers who played for the first team after coming through the academy?

15. In what country did Thierry Henry break the Arsenal goalscoring record?

Answers on page 61

16. Which Arsenal player scored in the 1998 World Cup final?

17. What nationality do Lauren and Alex Song have in common?

18. How many penalty shootouts were Arsenal involved in throughout the entire time at Highbury?

19. Who is the all-time leading scorer at Emirates Stadium?

20. Who was the last Arsenal player to score a hat-trick for England?

21. What was the first trophy Arsène Wenger won as Arsenal manager?

22. Who scored our first goal of the 2019/20 season?

23. What award did Jack Wilshere win in 2010/11?

24. How many goals were scored in total in the League Cup game against Reading in 2012?

25. From which club did we sign Rob Holding?

26. Who was our captain when we won the Premier League title in 1998?

27. What is the name of the main Arsenal merchandise store at Emirates Stadium?

28. What London postcode is Emirates Stadium situated in?

29. Which of these players have NOT played in an FA Cup final for Arsenal – Yaya Sanogo, Wojciech Szczesny or Carl Jenkinson?

30. Who is our all-time leading appearance maker?

31. Before Freddie Ljungberg, who was the last Arsenal manager to have also played for the club?

32. At which end of Emirates Stadium is the clock situated?

33. Who are the only two players to score for us in FA Cup finals while captaining the side?

34. How many Premier League hat-tricks did Thierry Henry score for us?

35. At which stadium did Julio Baptista and Andrey Arshavin both score four goals in a game?

36. What feat did Jermaine Pennant and Robert Pires both manage in a 6-1 home win over Southampton in 2003?

37. True or false, Thierry Henry was never on the losing side in a north London derby?

38. How old was David Seaman when he captained us in the 2003 FA Cup final?

39. What shirt number did Ian Wright wear on his Arsenal debut?

40. Which Arsenal player has the most Twitter followers?

PLAYER SPOTLIGHT

19
FWD

NICOLAS PEPE

BORN: MANTES-LA-JOLIE, FRANCE, MAY 29, 1995
NATIONALITY: IVORIAN
JOINED ARSENAL: FROM LILLE ON AUGUST 1, 2019
PREVIOUS CLUBS: POITIERS, ANGERS, ORLEANS (LOAN), LILLE
ARSENAL DEBUT: V NEWCASTLE UNITED (A) LEAGUE, AUGUST 11, 2019

Outrageously talented and tricky winger Nicolas proved a hit during his first season in England, regularly causing havoc when cutting in on his stronger left foot from his position on the right wing. The Ivory Coast international smashed our transfer record when he joined from Lille in the summer of 2019, and soon made his mark - most notably with a pair of superb free-kicks to earn a comeback win against Vitoria in the Europa League. An exciting, speedy forward who can also play centrally, he contributed 10 assists in all competitions during his debut campaign, including for Aubameyang's winner in the FA Cup final at Wembley.

PLAYER SPOTLIGHT

22
DEF

PABLO MARI

BORN: ALMUSSAFES, SPAIN, AUGUST 31, 1993
NATIONALITY: SPANISH
JOINED ARSENAL: FROM FLAMENGO ON JANUARY 29, 2020
PREVIOUS CLUBS: MALLORCA, GIMNASTIC, MAN CITY, GIRONA (LOAN), NAC (LOAN), DEPORTIVO LA CORUNA (LOAN), FLAMENGO
ARSENAL DEBUT: V PORTSMOUTH (A) FA CUP, MARCH 2, 2020

A loan signing during the 2020 winter transfer window, Pablo made his move permanent in the summer. An ankle injury kept him out of the end of last season, but before lockdown he helped the team keep clean sheets in each of his first two appearances. A powerful, intelligent central defender, the Spaniard had previously been on the books at Manchester City, but didn't make an appearance there before moving to Brazil. He won the league title with Flamengo, and the South American equivalent of the Champions League - the Copa Libertadores - before impressing in the FIFA Club World Cup final against Liverpool, shortly before joining the Gunners.

YOUNG GUNS

These three Young Guns all got a chance to show what they could do while out on loan last season, and they have returned home with extra motivation to shine in Arsenal colours.

JAMES OLAYINKA

Position: Midfielder
Born: London, October 5, 2000
Loan club in 2019/20: Northampton Town (League Two)

Classy midfielder James only played a handful of games for Northampton Town last season, but his appearances included the League Two Play-Off Final victory at Wembley Stadium. James started last season with Arsenal, and scored four goals from just 11 appearances for our youth sides, including one in the Checkatrade Trophy, in which we fielded an under-21 side. Ironically that came against Northampton Town in a 1-1 draw in the group stage, and a few months later he signed on loan for the Cobblers. He made just one league appearance before the lockdown, but they sneaked into the play-offs upon the resumption, and James played both legs of the semi-final win over Cheltenham. He then came on as a sub in the 4-0 final victory over Exeter at an empty Wembley to ensure promotion to League One. A versatile and dynamic central midfielder, James joined the Gunners when he was just six years old, and has steadily developed since then. Eligible to play for either England or Nigeria, he burst onto the scene in summer 2019 when he scored his first Arsenal goal for the first-team during the pre-season friendly win over Colorado Rapids.

DEYAN ILIEV

Position: Goalkeeper
Born: North Macedonia, February 25, 1995
Loan clubs in 2019/20: SKF Sered (Slovakia) and Jagiellonia (Poland)

An athletic and imposing goalkeeper, Deyan has been with us ever since 2012 when he joined as a teenager, and has been a mainstay of our youth sides throughout that time. But last season he gained first-team experience during two loan spells in Europe. The first was at Slovakian Fortuna Liga side SKF Sered. He was the regular first-choice keeper for the top-flight side, making 18 appearances and keeping three clean sheets, before moving on again in the January transfer window. This time he was heading to play in the top tier of Polish football, for Jagiellonia Bialystok - where he kept two clean sheets in his first four starts. An influential member of the Arsenal youth setup, Deyan played 17 times for our under-23 side during the previous season, and captained the side at Emirates Stadium. A highly-rated, modern-style goalkeeper, he has been in the Arsenal first-team squad as an unused sub - most notably for the 2019 Europa League final. He has represented his country at every youth level so far.

JORDI OSEI-TUTU

Position: Right back/right midfield
Born: Slough, October 2, 1998
Loan club in 2019/20: Bochum (Germany)

After making rapid progress in the Arsenal academy, Jordi stepped it up a level last season when he joined German second division side VfL Bochum. The attack-minded right back was an instant hit - playing at both full back and on the wing, impressing with his power, speed and technique, while chipping in with the odd stunning goal as well. In fact he was the first Englishman to score in any league following football's resumption after the coronavirus epidemic, netting in a 3-0 win over Heidenheim. Jordi first came to prominence at Arsenal when he was selected as part of the first-team squad on the pre-season tour to Singapore in 2018. He has also been on the bench for games in the Europa League, FA Cup and Premier League for the Gunners, but began the 2020/21 season still awaiting his first-team debut, having joined the club from Reading as a 16 year old.

WHO AM I?

The sooner you get it right, the more points you score!

PLAYER A

1. I was born on May 28, 1991 (5 pts)
2. I made my debut against Chelsea (4 pts)
3. I used to play for Lyon (3 pts)
4. I wear number 9 (2 pts)
5. I am French (1 pt)

PLAYER B

1. I was born on September 2, 1992 (5 pts)
2. I made my debut against Coventry City (4 pts)
3. I went on loan to Reading (3 pts)
4. I joined Arsenal in 2010 (2 pts)
5. I am a goalkeeper (1 pt)

PLAYER C

1. I was born on January 20, 1995 (5 pts)
2. I made my debut in the Community Shield (4 pts)
3. I joined from Southampton (3pts)
4. I wear number 21 (2 pts)
5. I have played for England (1 pt)

PLAYER D

1. I was born on July 28, 2000 (5 pts)
2. I scored my first goal against Qarabag (4 pts)
3. I have played for England youth teams (3 pts)
4. I came through the Arsenal youth system (2 pts)
5. I wear number 32 (1 pt)

PLAYER E

1. I was born on May 29, 1995 (5 pts)
2. I am left footed but usually play on the right (4 pts)
3. I am Arsenal's record signing (3 pts)
4. I wear number 19 (2 pts)
5. I play for the Ivory Coast (1 pt)

MY TOTAL POINTS:

Answers on page 61

COMPETITION

Answer the following question correctly and you could win an Arsenal FC shirt signed by a first team player.

Of all the players who played a first-team match for us in 2019/20, who had the highest squad number?

A) **Bukayo Saka**
B) **Gabriel Martinelli**
C) **Cedric Soares**

Entry is by email only. Only one entry per contestant. Please enter AFC SHIRT followed by either A, B or C in the subject line of an email. In the body of the email, please include your full name, address, postcode, email address and phone number and send to: frontdesk@grangecommunications.co.uk by Friday 26th March 2021.

DID YOU KNOW?

Here are some weird and wonderful facts about Arsenal. Use them to amaze your friends!

The most league goals ever scored in a top flight season for Arsenal was 42, by Ted Drake in season 1934/35. He reached the remarkable tally from just 41 games. It's a figure that no player, from any club, has since matched for a single season in the English top division.

Arsenal were the first English side ever to defeat Real Madrid and Borussia Dortmund away from home, as well as both Inter Milan and AC Milan at the San Siro.

Arsenal are the only side in the past 100 years to remain unbeaten away from home for an entire league season - and we did it twice - in 2001/02 and again two seasons later.

We jointly hold the record for playing in the highest scoring draw in English league history. Arsenal and Leicester shared 12 goals in a Division One game in 1930, while Charlton and Middlesbrough also played out a 6-6 draw in Division Two 30 years later.

The last time an Arsenal starting XI consisted purely of players born in the British Isles was on March 22, 1995 - away to Manchester United. From that day onwards, every Arsenal team has featured at least one foreign-born player.

The most common first name to play for Arsenal is James (or Jimmy) with 48 players so far.

Emirates Stadium took 123 weeks and two days to build, and opened with the Dennis Bergkamp testimonial match on July 22, 2006.

Six Arsenal players have won the World Cup while at the club: Emmanuel Petit, Patrick Vieira, Cesc Fabregas, Lukas Podolski, Per Mertesacker and Mesut Ozil.

We hold the record for scoring in consecutive league matches, netting in 55 games in a row between May 19, 2001 and November 30, 2002.

Defender Tom Parker once played in 172 consecutive fixtures for the club, not missing a single match, in any competition, between April 1926 and December 1929 – more than three and a half years!

BERGKAMP 10

We have won 13 league titles, and have twice clinched the championship at both Stamford Bridge and White Hart Lane, as well as once each at Anfield and Old Trafford.

Arsenal played an incredible 70 games in all competitions during the 1979/80 season, and still ended the campaign without a trophy. It remains the record for the most games played by a top-flight side, and midfielder Brian Talbot played in all 70!

The dimensions of the Emirates Stadium pitch are 105m x 68m.

Arsenal hold the record for the longest unbeaten run in English league football, avoiding defeat for 49 games between May 7, 2003 and October 16, 2004.

In addition, we hold the record for the longest unbeaten away sequence in the league, with 27 games from April 5, 2003 to September 25, 2004

A game between our first team and reserves was the first ever football match to be televised live, on September 16, 1937.

The fewest goals Arsenal have scored in a league season was just 26, way back in 1912/13 - it's the only time we have ever been relegated in our 135-year history.

Arsène Wenger won the FA Cup seven times – more than any other manager in history.

Arsenal have been represented by players from more than 60 different countries, including Lithuania, Algeria, Australia and Mexico.

The highest scoring penalty shoot-out in our history ended 9-8 to the Gunners, after 11 rounds of spot kicks. It came against Rotherham in a League Cup third round match at Highbury in 2003, and remains the only time we have ever had a penalty shoot-out in a home match.

Seven Arsenal players lined up for England in a friendly against Italy in 1934 - it remains the most players selected from a single club side for a national team game.

PLAYER SPOTLIGHT

23
DEF

DAVID LUIZ

BORN: DIADEMA, BRAZIL, APRIL 22, 1987
NATIONALITY: BRAZILIAN
JOINED ARSENAL: FROM CHELSEA ON AUGUST 8, 2019
PREVIOUS CLUBS: VITORIA, BENFICA, CHELSEA, PARIS SG, CHELSEA
ARSENAL DEBUT: V BURNLEY (H) LEAGUE, AUGUST 17, 2019

A seasoned campaigner in the Premier League, David enjoyed a fine debut campaign with us, becoming a mainstay of the defence as soon as he arrived from Chelsea near the end of the 2019 summer transfer window. A tough yet skilful central defender who can also play in midfield, the Brazilian has a wonderful eye for a pass, and often launches attacks from deep inside his own half. The world's most expensive defender when he joined Paris Saint-Germain from Chelsea in 2014, last season's FA Cup success was the 19th major honour of his club and international career – a tally that also includes the Champions League, Premier League and Confederations Cup.

35
FWD

GABRIEL MARTINELLI

BORN: GUARULHOS, SAO PAULO, BRAZIL, JUNE 18, 2001
NATIONALITY: BRAZILIAN
JOINED ARSENAL: FROM ITUANO ON JULY 2, 2019
PREVIOUS CLUBS: CORINTHIANS, ITUANO
ARSENAL DEBUT: V NEWCASTLE UNITED (A) LEAGUE, AUGUST 11, 2019

It was a stunning breakthrough season for Brazilian youngster Gabriel, who wasted no time in forcing his way into the side after joining as an unheralded 18 year old in the summer of 2019. Arriving as a winger, he soon showed he is also very effective as a centre forward, scoring seven times in his first four starts. He wrote more headlines in January, scoring in back-to-back Premier League games, including an unforgettable run from his own half away to Chelsea, followed by a cool finish. His season was unfortunately cut short by injury just after the lockdown, but he had already done enough to earn a contract extension by then. A superb dribbler with a work-rate to match his talent, the teenager has represented his country at under-23 level.

GREAT GOALIES!

Can you find these Great Gunners Goalkeepers?

```
M N O S L I W K P H F R
F F A B I A N S K I P O
Z J L R M C L B L W T L
E G E F E E F K E R A Y
N Y G N N G K A H I I A
I N F O N R N N M G N T
T Z M L H I L I A H U R
R X L C P R N V N T M N
A P E S P B L G N N L H
M C O C I K U L S F A H
F Q S E A M A N N R B M
L Y N S E Z C Z S H G H
```

Almunia   Lehmann   Martinez   Taylor

Cech   Leno   Ospina   Wilson

Fabianski   Lukic   Seaman   Wright

Jennings   Manninger   Szczesny

MISSING IN ACTION

Look at these six photos, and tell us who is missing in each one

Answers on page 61

JUNIOR GUNNERS

Junior Gunners is the Youth Membership scheme for Arsenal fans aged 0-16 years. Our JG Members receive access to a range of exclusive benefits, including:

• Opportunities to interact with Arsenal first team players.
• Access to free family events.
• The chance to go behind-the-scenes on a match day.
• Weekly competitions, with prizes such as signed player items.
• Access to the Junior Gunners app.
• An exclusive Membership Pack*.

There are three tiers of JG Membership; Welcome to our World 0-3, Team JGs 4-11 and Young Guns 12-16. Each tier has their own exclusive events and competitions.

Prices start at £10. To find out more and to join, head to arsenal. com/membership/junior.

*Membership Pack available to Full Members only.

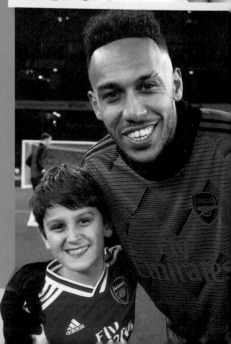

QUIZ ANSWERS

WHO'S OLDER?
1. David Seaman
2. Dennis Bergkamp
3. Robert Pires
4. Cesc Fabregas
5. Theo Walcott
6. Tomas Rosicky
7. Gabriel Martinelli
8. Kieran Tierney
9. Rob Holding
10. Bernd Leno

SPOT THE DIFFERENCE

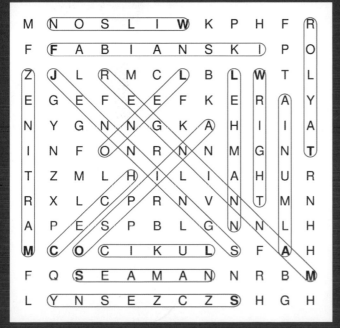

TRUE OR FALSE
1. False 2. True 3. False 4. True 5. False 6. True 7. True 8. False 9. False 10. True

WORDSEARCH

FACE SWAP
A. Gabriel Martinelli, Nicolas Pepe, Kieran Tierney

B. Bukayo Saka, David Luiz, Hector Bellerin

C. Bernd Leno, Granit Xhaka, Eddie Nketiah

WHO AM I?
A. Alexandre Lacazette
B. Emi Martinez
C. Calum Chambers
D. Emile Smith Rowe
E. Nicolas Pepe

THE GREAT BIG ARSENAL QUIZ
1. Alex Iwobi and Paul Dickov
2. Victoria Concordia Crescit
3. Old Trafford
4. Southampton
5. 14
6. 2006
7. Freddie Ljungberg
8. 7
9. O2
10. 2-1
11. Bournemouth
12. 1886
13. Cesc Fabregas
14. Hoyte
15. The Czech Republic
16. Emmanuel Petit
17. Cameroonian
18. One
19. Robin van Persie
20. Theo Walcott
21. The Premier League title
22. Pierre-Emerick Aubameyang
23. PFA Young Player of the Year
24. 12
25. Bolton Wanderers
26. Tony Adams
27. The Armoury
28. N5
29. Carl Jenkinson
30. David O'Leary
31. George Graham
32. South
33. Per Mertesacker and Pierre-Emerick Aubameyang
34. Eight
35. Anfield
36. They both scored hat-tricks
37. True
38. 39
39. 9
40. Mesut Ozil

MISSING IN ACTION
1. Aaron Ramsey
2. Leah Williamson
3. Thierry Henry
4. Mikel Arteta
5. Arsène Wenger
6. Olivier Giroud

SPOT GUNNERSAURUS!

WE BELIEVE IN THE ARSENAL
SENAL MACEDONIAN SUPPORTERS CLUB — Arsenal NORTH WALES (GOGLEDD C) — KEEP THE FAITH — 1987

Arsenal ICELAND — DEEP IN THE ♥

Fly Emirates to Dubai — The Arsenal Foundation — www.arsenal.com/thearsenalfoun

1886

FLY BETTER